"This is a little something for myself,

to clear my thoughts and consciousness."

...by Candlelight

Edited by Aaron and James Dalzell

Cover designed by Aaron Dalzell

ISBN: 978-0615948744

Other works include:

Forgemaster (2013)

...by Candlelight

Aaron Dalzell

My Thoughts:

"It's time for the Masquerade,

grab your mask, and don't be
late, light the candle,

and stay up late!"

The Maskerade Ball

~

A masquerade through midnight,
as the witching hour chimes upon the clock face,
A masquerade through war, and all the leftover bodies,
which lie dead and stumbling, are left alone upon the floor,
A masquerade through love, as the bodies intertwine,
as hot as the dragon's breath, as cold as hatred's deception,
A masquerade through hate, our fervor hate boils and over-
flows, and all dreams for the future turn to night, and our worst
nightmares, can still harm us in the long, dragged-out hours of
the daylight.

A masquerade of emotions, where a kiss turns to shove, and a
hug is murder, when the knife is driven into our backs,
A masquerade of darkness, as the sun fades and the night
crawls on hooves, on all twenty-four hours,
A masquerade of subtlety, of liars, cheats, crooks, and
backstabbers gather in this solitary space, where they may

cross one another, with that huge smile upon their face,
A masquerade of who I am not, and who I may yet be, am I
myself, am I you, am I me, who are you? Do you even know?
When the witching hour strikes, and we put on our masks,
we hold each other's hand, and we walk across the sands of
midnight, that place that only exists in the shadows of the
mind, for tonight we dine with the creatures of the darkness,
the people of the night, we party until the dawn,
with these strangers we tongue and lick, but we never liked,
we never even kissed.

Tonight is a special night, for this is a celebration of death and
decay, and mourning the loss, the precious life that has passed
away, a masquerade of time, as we watch the hours bleed away
like the passing of a stone, a masquerade of falling behind,
for you already know how painful it is to see the time passing
by, but now you're running out, and you can never get ahead,
when your falling sixty steps back,
A masquerade of a bitter sleep, for there is none to be had, the
sheets are wet,
covered with a guilty man's blood and sweat, tears that can

never be washed away, sheets stained with sadness and memories that will never go away, moments we have shared with someone we have loved, and the pain of their memory will never leave this room, nor that space we have given to them in our mind, and their ghost is there to haunt us until the end of our time.
This is a masquerade through my midnight mind, are you still there? Are you still alive?
Or are you just like all the others, and lost within this confusing mind?

But please don't despair, for this is a celebration without the final ecstasy, a party where no one shows, except for those with no path or destiny, and when I look around this empty room, I see you...I see me...
Love me...Hate me as you please, for it is the emotionless that cannot see, cannot understand, that without the changing of the midnight tide, we sit idle upon a lifeless sea, drowning, trying not to let go, trying to breath, and the party becomes uninteresting, that's when everyone leaves, bored and unentertained.

Does my ravishing thoughts and ideals entice you?
Do you run and flee, or sit a bit and stay with me?
Listen to me! Are you on my side of my mind, on my time?
Or are you my enemy, and wasting my time...
my time that was once for me?!
This is my party, my masquerade, and I shall behave as
I please, for I am your host...your master of ceremonies,
For I welcome you to the masquerade ball, so please sit
and enjoy the festivities, for I am your servant, you are my
slave, for I wear this mask of hospitality, but maybe my face
underneath is hostility?
Will you show me your true face...because I like your mask,
it suits you well!
It really does lie to you, and hides your true self...

Collapse

~

Our world is undergoing a collapse,

the entire population has fallen under its own weight,

to death and eradication, none are left to stand,

no more do we walk upon this free land,

the war has started,

is this the beginning of the end?

H.U.N.K

~

Hear the screaming of the metal,
as the shrapnel rains down from the amber skies,
feel the kiss of flame as it burns across the flesh,
see the darkness of the black clouding over,
before I'm buried under by this creature's blood-thirsty attack!

Hear the roar of the infernal destroyer,
feel his claws tear apart and gouge at the flesh,
and the bones of the skeletal structure shatter and break,
as the bombs and bullets rip apart the tissue and guts!
Limbs scatter, bodies retreat, but they can't escape,
the creatures rampage, they can't escape defeat!

Hear the pleads of all the dying,
young and old, innocent and guilty,
for no one escapes the nightmare creature in one piece!
Feel their sorrow, feel their pain, as we all rot within

the creature as bodily remains, and the land breaks apart,
brotherhood splatters upon the grass, with the blood of their
bodies, and this huge undying nightmare creature,
spreads its plague and famine, this huge undying nightmare
creature, spreads it's war and hostility,
this huge undying nightmare creature,
will never let us awaken, for we shall all sleep,
forever and ever, until it brings about...the end of time..

Tyrant

~

From a thousand year sleep, he has risen,
for a thousand years, he has reigned,
for even in death, his subjects have spread tyranny and pain.
The empire of blood, has once again risen,
the crown of flesh placed upon his brow,
eyes have been gouged, and fists slam against teeth,
for the tyrant no longer sleeps!

He builds his throne of bones with broken slaves,
and his armies amass against the world,
hordes that charge, wave after wave, iron-clad and death
bound.
In sweat and stench, of bile and splattered blood,
the dying will drown,
as they die slowly, with their guts disemboweled!

All shall be taken in chains,
all heroes have fled, now exiles, no hope remains...
for the tyrant...once again reigns...
For the tyrant's name spreads,
upon every tongue and every blood-spitting lip,
as their led to their execution, by the crack of the whips.

Cities fall, and civilizations burn away,
fires that blaze like a thousand suns,
as humanity is driven into the dirt,
and covered with salt to never return.
A barren wasteland of piled skeletons, and plague crawling,
upon its hands and knees, and we raise our hands,
and swear fealty...
to the tyrant, and his rule of dominion and anarchy...

And all shall be taken in chains,
forever...the tyrant shall reign...

Down the Leviathan

~

The serpents are lit,
the atrocity steers towards eradication,
the mission will succeed,
when the code red alarm sounds,
and the drowning screams gurgle,
as the carnivores and cannibals of the sea,
drag their bodies beneath,

down, down, down…into the ragging sea,
drown, drown, drown…beneath the waves,
were darkness sleeps,
death, death, death…beneath the blood tide,
death, death, death…struggle to breath, as they are buried,
taken into the deep, cold and blind.

Drag them down…swallow them whole,
deicide the god of the waves,

the Armageddon of the world,
the lamb has been chosen,
and at the strike of twenty-seven after one,
the leviathan will be sent down to the bottom of the sea,
along with her crew, the war-mongering diocese,
the bodies for the sharks, the blood for the beasts,
their souls trapped under the storms of the sea,
where coffins sleep, and life on land can never breath,

down, down, down…beneath the raging sea,
drown, drown, drown…under the waves,
were silence rests in peace,
death, death, death…to the leviathan,
breath, breath, breath…new life into,
a world conquered by tyranny.

The haul bursts to flames…and the tanker explodes to pieces,
of burning steel, and chunks of titanium,
rain from the gray skies,
molten blood of opaque sludge pollutes the sea,
and spreads outwards among the battle-waves,

great whites and krakens from the deep,
fight over the bodies, like siblings over rag-dolls,
urchins melt them away into puss and slime to be absorbed,
crustaceans grip their prey with a desperate vice,
of hunger and starvation,
the maw of Charybdis swallows the metal carcass of the
 leviathan,
while Scylla eats the flesh and crunches the bones
of her crewmen, as the beasts drag them,

down, down, down…beneath the blood-red seas,
drown, drown, drown…as their flesh is torn to pieces,
death, death, death…this is war time!
death, death, death…by slaughtering this enemy,
we breathe new life, into a world without tyranny!

Waif

~

It's the morning after, and I have no home,
nowhere to go, nowhere to run and hide,
the soldiers march down my block, one after the other,
they have conquered my country, burned my home,
and enslaved my people, for am I the only one left?
They comb the streets, burning and pillaging as they pass,
terrorizing and murdering, striking fear into our hearts,
before tearing them out,
machine gunning down those who flee,
there is no shelter to run to,
they've burned and destroyed those too!
"Help me someone, please help! What's a lonely child to do!"
They slaughtered my pets, my dog and cat,
they shot my parents point blank,
and the general, he held me,
he forced my eyes open and made me look,
made me watch... as their bodies fell to the concrete,

and left there to lay, with all the others,
as the tanks and artillery,
pummeled their bones, and splayed their flesh,
and crushed their bodies.
I cried for days, but this is war,
I had to move on, I have to be the survivor,
somehow, some way, for days on end I prayed, asking why,
why does it have to be this way?!
For the army passes, and the bombers fly over head,
heading for the city,
where the last resistance will make their stand.
I wait for them to pass, and make my way across the yard,
I see a gun, an M-16 beneath my bare, dirty feet,
the shells of the bullets lay scattered about,
much bigger than my toes!
I pick up the round, and look at it,
and I notice the bodies these bullets ripped apart,
laying piled in the street across from the yard,
I look at the gun, and I ask myself, I use my grown-up mind,
"do I want to add to this blood-shed, do I want to be like them,
and slaughter all of them, as they have done to me?!"

"Yes!" For the answer is not to difficult to think about,
and so I take the soldier's gun, it's heavy,
and hurts my scrawny arms,
but I'll get tough, I'll get tougher, I'll train myself how to use it!
For I am alone, against the enemy...I stand alone.
I find a helmet sitting nearby,
the paint has been burned away by flames,
I don't know whose side?
But I pick it up, and place it upon my tiny noggin,
It wobbles around my brow,
for it is far too big, for my little head,
but I'll grow into it, I'll get bigger, I'll get used to it,
and before ya know it,
it'll fit my tiny head, and they're blood will paint it red!
I hold the gun in both hands,
and turn to look at the army fading into the city limits,
down the road and miles away from me, and the shots ring out,
the battle for the city is just the beginning,
I look to my right, and see a piece of broken glass,
and as I move closer and look down,
into the broken pane, there stands the reflection,

of not a boy, but a man,

a man who has his answers, who knows his destiny,

a boy who has wiped the dirt from his face,

and has grown up to be the last of his race,

there stands a soldier, the last of his kind,

for this soldier is different than the others,

against hopeless odds, I am a survivor,

for the phoenix has risen once more,

and this boy has become the last hope, for this final war.

Vacant Ruins

~

Hollow are their voices,

yet if we listen carefully,

we can still hear,

about the destruction,

that brought about the past,

for they may yet be,

a reflection of our future,

that's to pass,

for the winds chill the fallen stones,

that crushes down upon,

our ancestors' bones.

Walked the Earth

~

Once there was a civilization,
that walked the face of the earth,
upon the soil of Gaia, many, many eons ago,
now their civilization has crumbled,
laying dormant in ruins, under forensic rubble.

Once there was a race of men and women,
and the bones of their children, who never became adults,
their museums displayed the artifacts of their past,
but who is left to display them?
For their future, has been laid to rest.

Once there was a land upon a vast, and endless sea,
many never had a chance, some had way too many,
some were guilty, some were never proven innocent,
but they never had a chance,
with the coming of the destructive tide,

A final breath, the last inhale of stale air,
now their time has passed.

Once there was a sacred planet,
the third jewel from the eternal sun,
But now, this place is a boiling sphere of gas and smoke,
and once upon this planet was a race,
now devoured by the tide of famine,
destruction, and nuclear war.

Once a race of human beings walked this earth...but no more...

"what waits beyond..."

~

And the figure in robes approaches the podium,

in a brave, somber voice he projects his speech,

and all gather round and all listen to his words, as he speaks:

"What waits for us beyond the portal?
What fear lurks in the dark recesses of our mind?
Does this feeling, this nightmare have a name?
Yes, my brethren, my flock...my gathering!
For it is the atrocity of the human condition,
the phantoms of doubt, and shattered love,
that fill us with this hatred,
that leads us down our darkened path!
Into the recesses of our darkened mind,
our altered conscious, that aspect of ourselves,
that we never wish to know...never want to find...!"

And the figure in robes steps down from the podium,

he takes off his mask to reveal his true motives,
the actions in which he takes to brainwash us,
to fill our heads with pretty speeches,
a fast talker, a cheat, a wolf in sheep's skin...A liar!
Who doesn't know the true distance,
from the sky above our heads,
down to the heels of his two left feet,
I cover my ears when he speaks,
he doesn't know what waits beyond for you or me,
because he doesn't know the people we are,
he takes no time,
to get to know the people he meets...
his brethren he cheats!

Penumbra Darkening

~

……….. ……………………………………………. ……??????

……..black……….have been my dreams of late…..

my sleep…..cast far above the blue skies…..as I orbit….

as I sail across…..these many layers of space…….

…..and….what waits out there….?

What has outlasted us….beyond the beyond….

And time continuum……….? I

…and these shining starlets dance for me……

To distract my mind from the ambush of calamity,

My whispers are heavier than this gravity surrounding……

….but nothing is pulling me……….I guess my own

habitat……

This is the way my planet is…..rejecting me?

……by letting my mind float….endlessly? Affinity for me?

……to feel the cold space air, will put my mind at ease,

perhaps….but the comfort of others…….warms me,

...........................the rays of the solar star,

.........the sun was never the beginning, but.....it's color is changing....

Is it the end? Does the orb of gas and fire face its coda.....?

I am destined upon this odyssey, this caravan across the galaxy,

to survive? To...carry on a message?

The spokesman of human kind?

To whom...or to what...I speak....?

.....these many lights outside.....like a city night,

when the sun has set,

and all is quiet...when the people have gone to bed.......

there are no more lights down there...no more do the light switches work...on the earth below....the powers out for good this time......

.....this kind of quiet......is a special kind of muffle.......

....a silence that no earthling or living being.....was meant to experience,

this vacuum absorbs the sound away from lips.....not even the dead could think out here.....

but one might feel lucky.....because I have no fear....and I take what I can expect....

because each and every light-year, every checkpoint.....

is not what I expect……

out here, galaxies are colliding….the planets are realigning,

but that's how the mind works isn't it…

yet we know more about the configuration of the planetary

settings,

than we do, our own sanity…our own individual thought

patterns coexisting,

how long we'll last...before we break............................

……these many light-years seem to come and go,

they pass me by,

I no longer know what the time is, nor do I care,

but I am aware,

that the smells...nothing...and the gamma rays....increasing....

piercing the metal craft,

and I watch the sun, sink behind the many rings of Saturn,

and dwarf beneath the mass.......

of Jupiter, it's red eye glaring like a Cyclops,

a one-eyed watch dog, the other was shot out.....

and what went wrong with number nine,

why did we abandon Pluto?

Why did we leave the smallest one behind?

Just like Zeus, we passed him to the underworld of all

knowledge and existence,

or maybe it was....

....Survival of the fittest? An evolution, or an absolution?

Did we know something we shouldn't?

...........This universe......it's so...so vast and colossal,

is there ever an end? Where was the beginning,

or is this the middle?

I'm drifting further outwards, to an infinity that defies all time,

to places that have never existed until now...until our pending meeting,

but who will be waiting, what will be standing....upon the edge

of their universe, to greet me, to back-stab me....... as they

show me........

their...untraveled galaxy of wonders and mysteries that provoke

our primitive minds,

of the questions we never had answers for,

and alien lands, glowing terrains, plains of violet sands,

oceans of red, poisonous atmospheres, magma instead of grass,

civilizations under amoebic seas? Possibly?

Skies of a sunburst flame...of a star that's nearly dead..........or

is being eaten away.....

a black hole is in my wake.....as well as in my sleep,
my visions...my nightmare that's haunting me.....
swallowing me!
Creeping up on me...........an abyss without any reckoning,
as to where I'll be...mentally or physically.......separated into
atoms and pigments......
what mutations, what creations of other gods and deities...will
be waiting...will be...hunting....preying...enlightening?
The airlock has been disturbed...."Is someone there?!"
Will the darkness finally reach full black...when the vacant,
nameless shadows, reach mine?
The shadows are sliding on down, further on the scale......
What is that reoccurring chill nipping at the back of my neck?
What is that feeling...of cold air? The smell....of a foreign
space...a distant world.... an odor I have never sensed before...
is their time to explain, before it's too late!
Has someone come to visit me...all the way out here?!
....could..........................
.............could this be it?
could this be the moment, the moment humans have been
waiting for?!

Will the invader..........show its true face, reveal.....itself to me,
here we are.......two intergalactic terrestrials......foreigners and outcasts from parallel badlands,
worlds that have suffered war and famine.....starvation..... exclusion,
upon foreign craft....traveling, an exodus to distant lands.....
hardened by genocide......escaping the slaughter of two worlds....
only to come face to face.......
..............................are we...are we fated to destroy one another?!
....here it comes......................
...................it's here!
and I feel my..................my air...................red lights.........
a siren............a warning's flaring................my air.....
..............the cabin density..............heavy........
chest is.............heavy...............
shadow.................closer.........closer............
it's.........getting...........closer...........
I........eyes........blur.....
cannot.......tell...........what
but............the......

the damn things..............they don't breath..............!

THEY DON'T...

BREATH..........OX.......Y.......GEN..............................!!!!!!

....

....

....

....

....

.

____

____

[*And thus....when two shadows, converge into one....the night is darkest...when the interpretation of our enemy has won....what is left to fight for...when our dead eyes....no longer see the morning, and our flesh....cannot feel the warmth of a dying sun...*]

I

~

I have many faces, but only one name,
I have many personalities, but I'm not insane,
I have so much pain, but I'm not hurting,
I have so much anger, but I'm not burning.

I have many goals, but I'm still focused,
I have many accomplishments, but I'm not
famous,
I have so much sadness, but I'm still smiling,
I've been damaged and hurt, but I'm not crying.

I've said some stupid things, but I'll keep
talking,
I've been put down, but I'm not stopping,
I've been held back, but I'll keep going,
I don't know everything, but I'm still learning.

I'm still so young, but one day I'll be old,
I do everything I can now,
before I'm dead and cold,
I have my own agenda, don't we all,
I do what gives me pleasure, you may not agree
with me.

But I am who I am, I'm odd and different,
I am what makes me a human being,
our difference is far between,
I is who we are, I is the person we became,
I cannot be changed, I have a title,
I have my own name.

I is just one letter--one person,
I is different for us all,
The I who I am, is not who you are,
You may know more, you may know less,

I've only come so far,

I don't know everything, about what's truly

right and wrong.

But maybe one day I will,

at least what's right and wrong for me.

But this poem could go on and on,

and I'm still living,

If your reading this...good,

but do what you need to do,

I have my own shit to do, don't you?

The Countdown

~

12-Epochs, 11-Eons, 10- Millenniums

9-Centuries, 8-Decades, 7-Years

6-Seasons, 5-Months, 4-Weeks

3-Days, 2-Hours, 1- Minute

.5-Seconds

0- Every moment counts, when every moment

ends, every moment passes, with every breath

taken in, every moment dies,

when all moments have passed,

then our time is up, when we breath our last.

So make every moment count,

make every moment last,

And all that's left are memories,

when the countdown has passed...

My Passing

~

I think about it sometimes, you know,

when there's nothing going on

or nothing to do,

I wonder sometimes… how will it happen?

How will it come to pass?

When will it all be over,

and I have taken my last breath?

I don't dwell on the idea;

it doesn't consume me

or affect my daily agenda,

but, you know…do you ever wonder,

about how or when you'll go?

The month, the day and year?

What if we did know,

that's the unsettling part of this whole idea!

What if we knew the exact point on the

timeline,
When our life would stop, and go on no more?
That dash marked upon our final day,
when we fill in the year we were born,
and the year we died,
and the reasons…the reasons why…why?
Could we change the future if we knew?
Could we improve our quality of life,
and denounce our bad habits,
would we even care anymore,
if we knew we were reaching the end of the
line, could we make the transition into that
oblong box, and move back in with our
Mother Earth?
Maybe I will become ashes,
and soar with the wind to my favorite place.
On that day, will it rain?
And the water cascade down the casket at the
site, as the Paul Bearer's carry me,

to my final rest,
Will the snow blanket the ground,
and my bones lay still and cold,
under frozen soil?
Would those close to me…miss me still?
Would my passing bring new life,
on that first morning of Spring?
Will the flowers grow upon my earth,
will the birds still sing?
Will the day be a crisp autumn,
as crisp as the apples used to bake a pie?
Will a tear be shed on the day that I die?
Will the light of Summer brighten that gloomy
day?
Oh, how depressing,
the Summer nights would be, if I knew…
if I knew this was the day.
Would I ask myself questions,
would I regret what I didn't do?

Or could I hold my head up high…
and be proud of what I've done?!
Would I stay secluded and depressed,
or go out and have a little fun?
One last "Hurrah!" before I'm done.
Would my story continue,
and live on in other's minds,
after I have reached "The End" or Fin?
Would the sadness of those closest truly mend?
I believe you know the answer to that,
we move on,
but we're never fully healed.
So why not just think about now,
and live in these moments,
as though time were standing still?
Well…time doesn't,
and it continues to spin upon an eternal wheel,
with or without us, it moves on and on,
so let's just tell those around us now,

while we're still alive, how we truly feel.

I can ask all the questions I want,

but I'll never get all the answers I need,

so I'll just keep moving forward,

and go along with the wheel,

at least until there's nowhere left to go,

and I'll just keep on living,

until my life is spent,

but I will always be forewarned…

of that day when my life…is forfeit.

Shadow of my Past

~

It's been a while,
since I've had the words to say,
but now I think it's time,
to celebrate my best friend,
for he's gone now,
but I still think of him every day.

He was a stubborn old man,
had his own selfish personality,
always wanted to eat,
didn't care what it was, just ate anyway,
then he'd stick his nose up when finished,
and walked away.

He was a tired old man, just laid there all lazy,
snored like a warthog,
grunted like the Eighth Wonder of the

World, but he kept his looks for his age,
stocky, dark, and handsome.
He was trouble when he was young,
liked to chase the chickens,
liked the outdoors, just to lay on his back,
his wiener warm in the sun,
he didn't want to play fetch,
this was his idea of fun.

He was a sore old man, had trouble walking,
but he was given a second chance,
his final days to feel just like a puppy.

He became a sick old man,
he had no more self-control,
so he went for one final ride in the car,
and we took him to that place,
where all the old pets go.

He was my best friend,
I didn't want to see him go,

and I'll never forget that final look,
in his brown eyes,
on that day when my buddies life,
came to an end...

Rest in peace Shadow,
maybe someday, we'll go for a walk again,
down that misty road,
in the morning sunshine's glow,
I have your leash,
and the earth keeps your collar,
safe with your bones...

The Pass

~

It seems like it was just yesterday,
When I was standing on this side of the yard,
and you were over there,
Mom put on my sweater and coat, before going outside,
that was the last time I passed the football to you.

We threw it back and forth for a while,
as the time passed by,
hard to believe it's been almost twenty years,
but it was something much more than that,
we were spending quality time, and when I asked my question,
you'd throw the ball back with an answer, a comment or two,
on what life will be like, what kind of man I would be,
this child standing before you.

What I should be ready for, what was in store for me,
any suggestions on your mind, you offered to me,

knowledge to help,
as I make my way down this road,
heading to the major leagues,
and grow up to be the star player,
you and mom always saw in me,
raised an All-Star,
but destined to become a Hall of Fame legend.

The football spirals, in an arch across the sky,
"ups and downs",
you said that was a symbol of how life can be great,
then take a sudden dive,
but if we catch the pass,
and carry our burdens forward to the end-zone,
we can score the winning point, before the game is over.

I stand here now on the morning grass,
and I think about those times,
I come to a realization, that those little moments,
are the ones that will last forever.
We don’t pass the football no more, but I’m glad we did,

I learned many things, standing on this side of the yard.

Maybe one day, I'll make my way over to your side,
where you stood,
and when I look back, there will be my legacy standing there,
waiting for me, standing now where I once was,
with arms open, for me to throw the football back,
and we'll spend time together, the way you spent time with me.
And I'll pass to them, all the wonderful things,
there is in life to see, the experiences we go through,
it's all part of our learning.

"Good catch son! Now pass the football back to me!"

Pathways

~

There lays a road, out there beyond,
and far, far away,
hidden beneath the cool trees,
where dusk keeps its secrets safe,
not too many people want to travel this
direction, others have no choice in the matter,
but hey, some do enjoy their walk.
What awaits them there?
Well…I don't know, they never do say,
"See for yourself!" They reply.
And so I proceed, I make my own way,
to that hidden place,
the secret realm within the trees,
that waits in the shadows, so far, far away.

And when I get there,
the path way opens up…for suddenly,

it becomes all too clear,
the writing on the wall is easier to read,
I pass through a place,
of knowledge and intrigue,
I see sights my eyes don't believe,
neither would your own,
but you have to come see! *"Hurry, over here!*
Come and See!"
The road begins easy enough,
but is fenced in and well protected,
there's not much room for exploration.
But as I travel onward, the trail widens up,
and the fence…is gone!
Yet the keepers of the trees,
they still watch, they still see,
the guardians see me onward,
until I am out of their line of sight.
So the road begins to darken,
and the warmth of the sun,
is far behind me now,
my way is as dark as night,

with no light…and no one to guide me down
my path,
I proceed along without fear;
I'll fight my way through this final trek!
Of a route so many before me have taken,
and before me lays,
this final stretch of land, endless, hidden,
kept to the shadows,
shrouded in a lifetimes worth of mysteries,
as it rolls ever onward,
I see nothing,
except for what my thoughts create,
and my actions uncover,
new faces, new challenges,
obstacles I have yet to endure,
feelings I have never felt before!
You see…that's the fascination which leads us
down this foreboding road,
for each pathway is different,
and we each achieve a different ending.
For that road before my feet, is my own road,

my path, my guide through,
these dark and gloomy woods,
and my feet keep me along,
down this somber trail, and up ahead of me,
I see that faint, flicker of light,
a dancing, alluring goddess,
all the way down the road, what was her name?
Hope? I believe was her name, but who knows,
that's just what's on my mind.
For this road is different to one and all,
for to each his own,
we all have our own lives, our own fate,
some roads are long and drawn out,
some roads shorter than others,
some roads will never be walked upon,
some never paved.

But am I done walking,
is my journey complete?
No, I don't think so, not yet anyway,
but who knows,

what waits around the next bend in the road,
what is the answer?
What is that mystery to life, that sleeps,
beneath the cool shade,
of these sacred trees?
What's out there waiting to be discovered,
waiting inside me, to be awakened?
I'm not really sure of my fate,
but I do know one thing,
when I've reached the end of this pathway,
I'll never be the same…

The Lady of Night

~

She stands alone, waiting in the corner of the dark streets,
waiting for another man to pass,
waiting for that prince in shining armor,
to sweep her off her feet.
They will pay her with gold and silver,
as she performs her acts of pleasure,
and then her clients will fade away,
and leave her to the night, as her
man in suit and tie, wife-beater and jeans, drives away.

But another body will come,
and more pleasure shall ride through town,
upon Porsche or Ferrari, no--more like a Chevy or dirty,
beat-up Ford,
with the paint chipping off and one headlight, covered in mud,
for it has been in need of cleaning, like her,
just a vehicle in the hands of her mistreaters,

she longs to be clean, she longs to be free,
for she has no lease, neither a title in someone else's name,
she is a human being!

But until her knight in shining armor drives through town,
she is owned,
she is bought when the client rolls the window down,
and then her skirt is rolled up, and she must obey,
she is a lady of the night, and her office,
is under the streetlight, and the sign says "open for business!"
She's here to please tonight...

The Tapes

~

Female Voice:

"I see people...as cattle,

women are the brood,

and men go to the slaughter,

I see animals wearing suits and dresses,

bovine going to dinners and lambs to Sunday churches,

these are nothing more than dolls I can play with,

prisoners for me to torture!

Pests that need to be exterminated!"

Detective:

"And you're trying to justify this behavior of yours,

by killing the innocent? Your mad! Your motives...

Make no sense! You're nothing more than a monster!"

Female Voice:

"Monster?! You dare call me the monster,

when we are all monsters! We caused the wars,

we caused dissension and separation,

the blood is on the palms of every man,

woman, and child's hands!"

Detective:

"Who do you think you are...to take a life, to decide whether someone is to live or die! Who are you to say such...terrible things!!!"

Female Voice:

"I...I am the form...that blood has taken, I am the blood of life-times, that has seen enough...dripped for far too long! And I am here to coagulate, and with the tides...wash us all away!

(giggle)

I am Red Barbie...I am, every wet dream of death...a fantasy, that has become...a reality....

(laugh)

And Innocent? Why detective,

I don't see people as innocent...

I see them as...kill-things!"

(This is followed by more hysterical laughter)

-Taken from the Red Barbie interview tapes,

December 5, 2013.

The Urban Legend of Red Barbie

~

Ten thousand shades of red,
for ten thousand devils at the base of her throne,
worshiping her, groveling at her feet,
licking the blood from her legs and toes,
of those she has slaughtered,
covers war in blood,
and sickness and famine in bile,
she, the queen of the night, the glimmering shadow,
cast from under a red moonlight,
the mystic aura of flesh and bone,
ageless and perfect, beauty she keeps timeless,
she builds her palace from the foundations of sex and ecstasy,
and leads them in one by one,
the sirens call, the piper's flute,
a sweet lullaby, a lyre of the liar,
and like rats they follow, the blood she swallows,
she bathes in the sweat, they smell her sweet scent,

and that's when the red wine flows, and the burning stars,
no longer show, like rain that drips from the flower's petal,
and ripples into the still cold water,
on the dark-side of the rainbow,
a place where rain burns, her land where lives never return,
the lamps reflect upon the drowning man,
in the crimson puddle,
down the darkest corners of the avenue,
where they never saw, there were no witnesses in view,
he never saw her coming, he never had a clue,
that's where she waits,
that's where she catches the flies that pass,
within her web of terror, her ancient lair,
a wisp of red lighting, is the color of her hair,
there is no warning, when she's right there,
when she smiles, teeth of perfect ivory,
lips that burn with the shade of her fiery glare,
so when you're out late at night,
standing beneath the stale city air,
waiting by the street light, for your expectations,
to by fate appear, and carry on with your evening, beware,

just remember one thing, and take special care,

I don't need to remind you of the urban legend of Red Barbie,

when she's already standing right there....

Love Never Dies

~

A jewel of the night approaches me in my sleep,
Who covers her face, as she weeps,
I ask, *"A sweet kiss, dear lady...*
And my thoughts are yours, and my life...is forfeit."
And as I gaze into those ruby eyes,
I forget who I am, who once...was I?
For by her love...I am petrified...

She a silhouette, draped in sensuality,
as she beckons to me,
calls to me, her voice so sweet
and innocent, one that would never harm me,
but wraps her arms around my shoulders,
and would forever embrace me and my dreams.
She says:

"I offer you ascension, to rise above all time and infinity,
you will have the knowledge of lifetimes,
past, present, and future.
I offer you a second chance, plead to me, and from this pain,
I will set you free, living is a nightmare, but a nightmare
can feel as good as a fantasy, I can turn your pain into ecstasy.

For I know what it is you so truly desire,
I offer you my hand, for friendship everlasting,
A kiss of love, that is undying, my blood in your veins,
drink of me, taste of my fresh lips,
we will writhe in passion, for love is only gratification,
I offer you eternal passion, drink of me
and your ascension will be complete.

For love never dies, when our bodies meet,
I want to feel your lips upon me,
run your tongue down my spine,
as I cry, as I moan and whine!
A mouthful of blood, a kiss, the taste of iron,
your lips are warm against my cold flesh.

You swallow hard, for the blood runs thick,

your closer to immortality, all it takes...is one last sip..."

Face in the Candlelight

~

I turn to the shadows,

I feel her presence; I feel her thoughts around me,

I know she's watching from the corner, playing with my fears,

She's taunting me!

I hear her whisper; her voice puts me in a trance,

her unhallowed shrill echoes in my mind!

I remember all too clear, that horrible autumn night she died!

She fell into the river, taken by the rapids,

her bones and body crushed by the rocks,

her agony…she scratches the walls,

her pain…moans echo in the halls,

of our house we built…the house, in which she still resides,

she always blamed me…she never forgave me,

for letting her fall.

She means to keep my soul, to drag me to hell with her!

I hear those footsteps…I hear the black water,

dripping on the floor!

The patter of her feet across the boards,

I break the spell, and cast light to the shadows,

and there she stands, her face in the candlelight…

A Lover's Embrace

~

Love twists, and coils around your spine,
As the lust is driven deep and the juices of intimacy,
seal our fate, with the immortal embrace.
Tears of inebriation flutter from the eyes of the divine,
ecstasy, a feeling of grandeur,
on a level that cannot be reached.
For mortal love is but a fling,
a play with a beginning, middle, and end,
but this love is everlasting without time and place.
A moment forever,
a kiss beyond passion's cloud in the heavens,
as an abomination we are seen,
but to be caught only heightens the release,
for I don't care, and you don't care, except for you and I…
And immortal our companionship, and forever our love will be,
even beyond the days we die.

A Dream of Rain

~

Tonight I see her again,

from an omniscient point of view,

she dances for me, in a dream of rain,

yet the water never touches her,

has her skin been burned?

Tonight she cries to me,

her eyes full of thunder and disdain,

she yells for me, calls my name,

lost in this dream of rain,

under the dark skies of this desert,

where her spirit remains,

can she ever leave, or will she always remain?

Tonight I want to save her,

but when I approach, she simply fades away,

was she never meant to be?

For I can barely see her,
lost in this dream of rain,
is she a figment of my imagination,
or my insanity?

The clouds brood over my mind,
and the lightning kisses her,
upon the dry, cracked skin,
the flames ignite,
but do the fires blaze for true passion,
or is her yearning the meaning of pain?
Will the feeling, the rush of water,
ever wash her sadness away?
Or shall I be greedy, and keep her to my mind,
where she'll remain?

Tonight it's lonely within this desert,
and the rain forever pours,
or is this rain simply my bitterness,
taking on yet another form?
The form of a storm, which forever rages!

Maybe if I let her go, this storm would end,
so green grass can grow,
and bring new solace to the bitter sands.

But for tonight, I think I'll let her dance,
for it's hard for me,
to break this infatuating trance.
And if we keep letting this storm,
fall forever on and on,
then we will both drown together,
and loose ourselves in this dream of rain...

A Harsh, Cold Winter...

~

A shiver runs down my spine,
when I see the brood of clouds,
trace your steps, follow in your wake,
its gonna be a cold, winter's day isn't it?
You bring in the icy wind,
leave me naked out in no-man's land,
you let the winter freeze my flesh,
and take away the warmth,
you lay the ice on thick,
I begin to crack, and break away,
your feelings for me were cold,
my hatred a burning fever,
and now I begin to melt away,
left a puddle, and I evaporate into nothing,
but I'll return with the spring rain,
to be reborn another day.

She Leaves in my Wake

~

I come back from the dead;
my spirit has arisen from a somber sleep,
I want to see her beauty, for she is the one I have missed,
I want to hold her close,
to warm my frozen bones with her love,
but she is not here with me, for she has forsaken my memory,
she is running out the front door, to another man perhaps?
The gold and orange leaves fall to the path, as she rushes past,
I guess my death has been a blessing,
for she no longer has my soul to keep,
she is free now to go, to move on to another as she pleases,
and to leave me here, as I awaken from my sleep,
to weep for the loss of my love,
who never wept for the loss of me…

Away (I)

~

I never understand why,

these things have to happen,

why they have to be this way,

I never realize when things go wrong, until it's too late,

and how do I make things right? No one ever explains that part.

Can I still speak to you?

Or should I just keep my distance?

Should I tell you how I feel…no?

Then I guess I'll keep my lips sealed.

And then you'll never know,

And I'll express the feelings I have for you,

to someone else.

Does it help, having you on my mind?

Does it help me heal the pain?

Does it confuse me, the way your memory drives me insane?!

I guess so; why else would I think this way!?

Do I still need to see you? Keep you in my sight?

Does it help heal my pain…well, it just might.

Can I keep you out of my mind? Can I leave our past behind?

No…I cannot, for your roots grow deep,

deeper than you may think.

You're there, and then you're gone in a blink,

yet I still need to hear your voice, I still want to hear you,

I just want to hear you say,

"I'm still around; I'll be here for another day."

I just don't want that bye, to be a goodbye,

I don't want you to go away…

Reconciliation (II)

~

I don't look back to those dark times we had,
a past that twisted us, and nearly destroyed our awakening,
but now...now I understand, do you as well?
now we must look ahead, for I don't look back...
don't look back anymore,
I'm ready for a new morning,
I'm awakening from the night before,
I look over to you, and you look back at me,
what are you thinking right now, are you awakening as well?
Your eyes are red, your lips dry and cracked, the color faded,
my body aches, my heart feels as though it were torn out,
wretched away from this sacred place,
the place where I held you dearest,
but I will heal, I will mend...if I say it,
just one time, could you heal too?
Can we reconcile?
Can we move on from this bitter sleep we had together?

Or are there better places for us...new faces...
higher places we may go?
If we were to part ways, could we continue to grow,
or will these memories hold us back,
keep us in a moment we once more, wish we had,
or is this a moment we will forever regret?
Do we have our own lives we need to follow?
Can we come to an understanding of what it is we truly want?
That this wasn't a nightmare, but just a bad dream, a mistake,
perhaps a small tear in the seams,
is this moment something we can mend?
Why don't we just hold each other's hand, and together,
we can turn one more page, and see where the story goes,
and follow the plot, as it twists and bends,
If I say I'm sorry...and that I love you,
do you love me? Can we make amends,
before our romance comes to an end?

Another (III)

~

Who were they, what were there names?

What betrayal have they caused...

what atrocities were afflicted upon you?

(Or was it always just you?!)

To make you feel such hate towards me!

(Or do you just hate, because I know you do!)

What is this severe trauma you hide,

what demons do you resurrect from your past,

when you see my face?!

I ask, because I just want to help...

but you'll never put your fists down.

(Don't you want to...isn't this confusion eating away at you?!)

What is there to say, to regain your trust? *(Nothing!)*

Would the silence be quieter, if you just opened up? *(NO!)*

But this hatred you keep, you hold onto from your past,

the misery and hurt caused by your many suitors,

you point it outwards,

into a missile, a ticking-time bomb about to explode,

you place this bomb at my feet,

then you dare laugh when it explodes,

and my feelings and peaceful nature are torn asunder,

(Or is it you that laughs at you,

is my pain a reflection of what happened to you?)

You verbally beat me down,

you scream about others when I'm the only one around,

(You lost your humanity, hardened and distraught,

you'll have nothing left to loose,

except a friend who tried to stand by you...

who gave up time... to try and save you,

to pull you through! But now I'm letting go,

you can swim or drown...your choice, you're on your own!)

I don't deserve your hatred!

(How would you feel? If you had anything left still...)

Why are you so mean...I never harmed you,

I don't want your hate, nor will I accept your love!

(For I have none left to give to you!)

I just want you to leave! Leave my memories,

for I no longer want to see or think of you!

Just...stay away from me.

(Get away from me...don't look at me so confused,

like it's all me!)

I read your thoughts when I see your face,

I know you've grown sick of me,

for there is another in the picture, there's no place left for me.

(I've been replaced, like a toy that was broken,

and a spoiled brat always craves what's hot and new,

but if it's perfection that suits you,

I'd say "Darling...your screwed!"

Nobody can do exactly what you want them to.)

But maybe I'm wrong...maybe he can make you feel great,

to put you on that pedestal, to make you feel like a princess,

the queen on top is what you want to be,

but you're not dainty...nor are you pristine,

your words are ugly and obscene,

and my attraction to you was my own fatal mistake,

like a tarnished, worn chalice filled with poison,

a bitter taste with a sweet, alluring smell,

to lure me into your web,

and suck all the blood from my mortal being,

and leaving nothing more than an empty shell,
of what I used to be,
you were afraid I would hurt you,
drive the stake into your tiny heart,
like all the others did, and you'd be left alone once again,
but maybe I'm wrong, and this horrid picture I draw of you,
is all overblown,
maybe you'll find happiness,
and you'll be satisfied after all is said and done,
settled down and the odds have evened out,
(Yet my mind still doubts!)
Time is not on your side, and love was never on mine,
I was doing time, but I'm free...
and you still remain a slave to the grind.
Another time perhaps? No, I'm over these nightmares,
these bad dreams I no longer have,
for I no longer think about those dark times,
those troubled dreams we had the night before,
your moved on, for another has been chosen,
as a slave to do your chores,
to be the one who receives the whip,

the one you've bound and drag with you,
as you follow your own road, I won't see you off, away you go,
yet, when all is said, it will never be done. *(Will it?)*
If you can be happy, then I would congratulate,
that another has done,
what so many have tried before,
what seemed like an impossible labor,
the thirteenth for Heracles,
but even he could not be that perfect man,
you hold within the gutters of your mangled day-dreams,
but what about me, I bet you don't care, or so it would seem,
but I'm gonna speak anyways, because I want you to listen,
I want you to realize...I want you to truly see,
that I thought this was a beautiful dream,
a ride of ecstasy, that would last for all eternity,
but like the lame animal, this dream was put to sleep,
my wish for us never did come true,
you were afraid of being the victim, me hurting you,
yet you turned this mess all around, and twisted it,
this romance now scarred and tainted,
you broke the golden rule...

"and did unto me, what I never would have done to you..."

yet, the good news is, I have moved onward,

I no longer cry for her...I no longer miss her.

Bad Blood (IV)

~

I tried...I tried so hard, but you treated me wrong,
so I keep the hatred alive, I keep these grudges strong,
you said some nasty words,
the truth hurts, but lies are worse,
I thought we were lovers, I thought we were friends,
I couldn't please you, so I guess I'm not worth a damn!
There are no second chances, when you lie and scheme,
there's some bad blood between you and me.

I have a pack of matches, and I burn another bridge,
and if there's one fact I'm sure of, you weren't the one for me,
douse the boards in gasoline,
but the fumes it gives off aren't clean,
a poison when I breath them in,
I guess this is how all feelings end,
the bitter thoughts we keep to ourselves, implode to do us in,
within the swirling charred clouds, I see your familiar face,

you're a cloud of noxious, hot air, and I see right through you,
my memory of you, a brief puff of smoke,
that blows away with the wind,
a forgotten memory, a sanction that bears no repeating,
for the hurt is planted deeper than a seedling,
your old and out of fashion, no longer worth anything,
you've been thrown away, not wanted by anyone,
I guess your nothing special it seems,
there's some bad blood between you and me.

How much deeper can you bury the knife,
into a wound that's sore from your insults,
scarred by this pain your causing,
how much more blood can you bleed from me,
I've never hated another so much,
I just want to be free!
I want nothing more, than for you to leave me be!

I'm moving forward, I'm never looking back,
I'm so insecure now, I have to plan my moves carefully,
and be aware of future threats,

I have my own plans, I know who I am, and what's best for me,
there was never anything between you and me,
there was no love, there was never a plan,
just a broken record, same excuses, same old song and dance,
I was never anyone, I was never your man,
you have so many fella's, cause you think you're the shit,
but if there's one thing I know for sure, you ain't worth spit!
Once I was hurt, twice I was sad, three cheers, now I'm glad!
but you could care less, because you'll do it to another man,
karma's gonna give you what you deserve,
I got what I want...I'm free!
Yet there will always be bad blood between you and me.

Ten years could go by, and we pass each other on the street,
our eyes won't meet,
they do, but we pretend not to see,
how long has it been since you thought of me?
I don't care, cause I don't think of you,
I can tell by that pissed off look, your drowning in misery,
that's fantastic news, because there's still,
bad blood between you and me.

Scratches and Bruises

~

Scratches and bruises,
mistakes with no bandages,
these tattoos are real and they bleed,
these scars upon me,
they're permanent and etched in stone,
to remind me of when I failed,
when I caused chaos and confusion,
disappointment and dismay,
for myself, there's no chance for healing,
the cure is already lost,
I never asked to be hurt,
when all I do is sacrifice,
all I do is for everyone else,
and at the end of the day,
I lick my wounds,
and the pain carries deep like an infection,
the puss erodes with bitterness,

I want to avoid pain, but I can't stay away,
from someone who needs me,
then turns their back and leaves me slain,
abandons me,
after all I did, when I was there to save,
when no one held your hand, I did,
no one identified with your pain,
I took it all away from you,
I did.
I absorbed your sickness,
I swallowed your poison,
and I lifted your world,
I held it on my shoulders,
and carried the weight,
of your burdens and mine,
I lend a helping hand,
and then get stabbed from behind,
just once would someone show me,
the love I show them,
just once I want to help,
without getting bitten upon the hand,

I just want others to be happy,

to have positive thoughts in mind,

I just want to be loved in return,

I just want to help, and be myself,

for I'm one of the few,

who have a heart and understanding,

I am one of an extinct kind…

Altar of Bodies

~

Bring yourself upon the altar,

of swinging blades and battle swords,

surrounded by pits of metal spikes,

where iron jaws upon your flesh, feast and gorge,

slinging pendulums and torches to guide your path,

as axes and maces swing with wrath.

Behind the altar, against the stone wall,

the family of our gathering sleeps peacefully,

and lay upon one another, like bound flakes of melted snow,

gray as the ashes of old.

Here only the dead lye, for all men, women,

and children we keep,

there is no sound, for within this place,

our bodies lay in pieces, but in peace, our souls sleep.

Bound by love, we give our flesh freely,
for the altar doesn't discriminate, for it loves us all dearly,
with its warm embrace of fresh, hot blood on metal and claws
that wrap around and tear at our flesh with a loving embrace,
oh how we are loved, and we will never leave this place.

There are no wars that cause pain, no one fights or rapes,
for if they did, their bodies would be piled upon ours,
for within these walls, in death, we are all equal.
Meat is just meat, and ours is no exception,
but we are not cows or poultry,
no branding or scarring we endure,
for the altar is sweet and kind,
its affection and sympathy we adore.

Our lives were meaningless,
but our death shall heal and cleanse,
for our eradication is necessary,
for true survival is our extinction.

Fear not the crude nature of the axe,
or the lifeless edge of the blade,
for they are here to serve and carve their way...
to a better living for them,
and a peaceful death for you and me.

Do not fear, for death is satisfaction,
the feeling of dying is gratification,
for we no longer feel pain, and no more do we grieve,
for the altar gives us the happiness we need.
Dying is not an option, it's a gift to be unwrapped,
deep within the forests, under the snow-laden tress.
So rejoice, and give thanks, for the best way to do so...
is to give yourself, to the altar of bodies.

Mirror

~

I take a deep look, into the eyes of a man,
a man I barely recognize anymore,
I cannot fool him, and he cannot fool me,
for we are one the same,
but there is something different,
he's not the man he was yesterday.

Has he matured, has he grown old,
does he keep secrets that need to be told?
I take a deeper look, but he won't look back,
he avoids my eyes, afraid to make contact.

"Speak to Me!" I ask,
but he will not answer, if he needs help, all he has to do is ask,
but when I look at him, and he...at I,
there is no one around us, in no one can we confide,
for there is only the two of us.

But can I trust him, for he does not trust me,
but we are one... he and I,
If we cannot trust ourself, then who can we trust?

His words sound so foreign,
a new language I barely understand.
He says such odd things, words I barely comprehend,
and neither does anyone else, is he still himself?
How can I possibly confide within this reflected man?

If only he spoke true, at least enough of himself,
and for me to understand,
for now, I finally realize the odd looks I receive,
for he glares it back at me as I speak,
I won't trust him, for he is no longer a friend to me.

Take these words to heart, from one who is lost,
within a reflective sea of thought,
when you no longer recognize yourself,
then how can anyone else...?

b00twerk

~

I feel as though this vast wall stands in my
way, and the more I try,
the higher I climb,
I just can't seem to overcome this obstacle,
that stands in my way,
I just want to take the sledgehammer,
and pound this wall down!
Then bulldoze the rubble away,
my rage is like dynamite, can't put a crack in it,
my fists like wrecking-balls,
that doesn't break it down,
my voice is supersonic,
that doesn't seem to harm it,
can't destroy it!
This wall will not go away!
What lies beyond this vicious exterior?
Accomplishment?

Goals that have been achieved?

I can't see over this barrier,

I don't know what lays ahead of me?

This wall…it blocks my path,

this wall blinds my true identity,

this wall separates my true self, from reality,

from the outside...

"I want to go outside and play!"

Why can't this wall just go away!

I just want this wall to go away!

I want to burst through this wall, to get away,

I want to burst through this wall,

and pave my way,

break this wall, and be on my way.

I'm tired of my life stopping in its tracks;

I just want to live,

and yet…I did want everyone to go away,

for we can't destroy what we've created,

for I am the architect,

I am the only one to blame,

for this wall's existence,

I have built it up, brick by brick by brick,

I've laid the foundation, I've walled myself in!

Now I want out, but there is no escape,

there's no way to break through,

this wall within my wake…

Face in the Earth

~

It's raining on my back again today,
am I still a person, if I bleed, will the blood,
soak up in the sand,
or wash away in the stream,
a constant flow that turned out different,
than I was lead to believe,
life's not what it seems,
life's never what it seems,
I'll just bury my face in the dirt,
I'll hide my shame and broken pride,
and all my secrets...
I'll tell them to the earth,
I'll keep safe in her womb,
in the darkness, covered in soil,
draped in her warmth, this is my safe place,
feeling the warm soil of the earth,
upon my face, a happy place,

tranquil to zone out,
out there beyond time and space,
buried deep, wash away my pain in the dirt,
I have those images, but never the names,
I'm just a tad bit scarce of what I truly need,
because what I have here,
isn't necessarily the best for me,
for life never is what it appears to be,
it changes its mind and memories,
what we want to see, what we want to be,
what is it we truly need? To be satisfied...
To be content...happy.
I appear in front of you, what is it,
that all of you as a group, truly see?
Do I leave an impact,
or am I simply a fallen tree,
cut down without a past, without a name,
the roots pulled out and tossed away,
over the hill to roll away,
slain in the woods, the day others came,
left in the dark, never noticed,

never seen,

and still I feel the rain falling upon me,

a broken stump, only half the man I should be,

cut down, and only a piece of me remains.

I socialize, to become one with the others,

but I carry the name they can't remember,

the face they soon forget,

but a name is just a name,

and a face is lost in the crowd,

mine... I bury in the ground,

where I cannot hear, I cannot see,

there is no sound, except my thoughts,

but there is a face,

there is someone with a name,

who buries away his shame,

someone who buries away the pain,

and always returns to his safe place,

to hide from his public shame.

Hoarder

~

These walls surround me,
these walls protect me,
I won't let them in, I refuse to let them in,
But I cannot breath;
I suffocate logic and sanity,
who knows what atrocities,
rest beneath the pile?
For only I know,
what secrets lay beneath the skin,
and when I clear away the filth,
should I let them in?
I will never let the memories go,
never let the grudges die!
For the nightmares are here to stay,
for in my disgusting sleep,
the nightmares will never go away!
These walls, they burry me…these walls,

they hide me…

and I begin to disconnect…

as my existence is carried away…

In a little box of garbage,

my grudges are stored away…

I am the Horse

~

I drag this plow through a cold, hard life,
I sow these seeds of anguish from grudges,
I cover for everyone's laziness,
as I pull my coffin closer to the grave.
I carry the burden of guilt upon my back,
I neigh; I bite the leather hard,
they pull harder at the reins,
I'm trying to communicate, trying to reach out,
to get someone's attention.
I carry the weight of the world,
upon my shoulders, as I continue my climb,
up this somber hill, under dark and heavy skies,
I see loathsome eyes gawk,
as they all keep their distance,
the pain I bear, must be infectious.
I've carried enough, I can't handle anymore,
but the problems just keep getting piled on!

And just like the beast of burden,
I pull…I keep pulling on.
Just like a helpless child, I scream,
I whine to get your attention!
Help me someone,
doesn't anyone have a solution?
Help relieve this heavy load from my back,
help me let my troubles go,
I keep dragging old baggage from my past.
If I'm approached as a friend,
I promise I won't attack,
I just want someone to help me,
to get this heavy burden off my back!

A Hero No More

~

Once…I used to be on top of the world,
I flew on the mystic wings of opportunity,
I was in the good graces of all around me,
…and I felt loved, I felt wanted,
I was seen as a hero,
I was counted on to be there,
when moments went wrong,
when the situation went sour,
but those days are long gone,
for I have fallen from above,
from the space where the moon meets the sun,
and infinity resides in between,
and my opportunities were endless!
I was once the nice one, a lover, a joker,
a savior, a provider,
I was…hope, in someone else's life;
I was beautiful in their eyes,

but no more, for I have hit rock bottom,
and my fall was crippling,
never to rise back up, never to be redeemed,
never to be forgiven by those around me,
now they are gone,
to be with others they deem worthy.
I'm at a point now,
where there is nowhere left to go…
nowhere I can go,
no lower could I possibly fall,
for I may as well have died,
for my life is below the bottom of the barrel,
and to get to me...
just turn the barrel on its side,
and underneath the muck and scum,
you will find…the shell of a confused, broken,
and crying man…curled up as a ball of string,
frayed, unraveled and exposed,
naked and opposed.
Who am I?
Well... if you must know,

I'm no one anymore, I suppose...

The Forgotten Man

~

Penniless, poverty stricken, an old homeless
beggar, what more is there to say?
Pornographic to the eyes of wealth,
and those fortunate enough to care.
Destitution, insufficiency,
reduced to drunken emptiness, just one coin,
and this wolf at the door will go away!

Possessions and lineage have been wrenched,
and severed from me,
alcoholic remedies heal this mind.
Cast upon this wasteland of barren streets,
to be cursed by those who pass.
"You're on the wrong side of these tracks,
crawl back into that hole where you belong!"

My life is that insignificant clump of dirt,

underneath the nail of mankind.

Cast down into ruin,
skin that bleeds from the bitterness of society,
erased from life and consciousness,
more and more each day.
A forgotten man wasted away,
but I did choose my own path,
and on cold pavement is where I sleep.
Tired, wasted, kept a prisoner,
inside my cardboard box of pain,
and that torturing smell,
of the nearby hot-dog cart, is here to stay.

Twisted, dementia,
things could have been different,
if I didn't give up so easily.
Mind constantly scolded,
by the waste left behind,
from the greed of society,
in these cylinders of treasure.

Gatherer, collector,

this taste of not being wanted I can relate,

The reality of having to beg for your life,

is pure hypocrisy!

baBB13

~

There isn't a clock on the wall,

not a single digit, not an hour or minute,

I know the time is there...I can smell the sweaty palms of the hands,

they're nervous, their anxious...just like us,

or me I mean? LOL!

I see the writing with the big pencil and the magic pen,

a text in my head?! Yes, I'll reply!

[2 L8 4me w/ Ma=eye=(o) iN~san it~E]

the walls glow in the dark, or maybe its radiation,

there's a sickness, a conspiracy going on here,

but it looks so nice to me, like Sunday's helping of ice cream!

I feel my mind racing, on two hairy legs in basketball shorts,

and knocked knees, a zigzag run it seems,

I see that check point ahead, as the sunshine rises in the west,

and sets in the east, it's not backwards, like my pants,

I can't see my feet underneath,

only my talons when I fly over seas,
where the hurricanes strike the Pacific Oceans in my western hemisphere,
stirring the calm, and disturbing the peace,
Piece??? a piece of pie the waitress brings me,
is it lunch time, or shall we fast forward to dinner,
you know! Run for the dinner bell,
take the escalator to the tower!
Did you bring the animals their food?!
Or maybe they forgot to use their brains and had to walk,
on all three, plus one cane,
Brains! None for me thanx,
I can't seem to remember which nightstand,
I sat mine on, or maybe it was boiled in the witches pot,
is that why it smells like an oven-baked forest?
Did I take the time to walk out the third door,
and forget to close it once more?
Or was it the last one on the right?
Did I take a wrong turn again, it's too dark up here to hear,
I sure could use a light, but it's night time at noon anymore,
but I can still hear the birdies chime,

they really sat the clocks back this time,

I can't see to put on my new coat,

"Nurse! Nurse! Is my jacket on straight?"

"How often does time slow down?"

~

Time?

Who has it anymore?

I don't know, I don't bother looking,

nor do I ask for it,

where did it go, since when has it been?

When's the last time you've seen it?

When's the last time you've had any?

How long has it been, how long will it be?

Does it even exist, is it physical?

Like a clock or a watch, maybe an alarm,

is it spiritual like a miracle,

but no miracle keeps time from passing,

stops dying,

because no matter what we're doing,

the time is moving,

the gears in the clock are whirring,

the batteries in my watch are dying,

the alarm is beeping,

I guess I'll wake up, because awake or asleep,

the time is passing,

and just how often does it slow down?

"...NEVER!"

Closer than they Appear

~

There's so many things I want to do,
but there's no time to accomplish them,
I could have five lifetimes,
maybe one hundred would do?
The mind, I used to think, was without limits,
but time and time again,
as I forget something old,
I've been proven wrong,
my body can't keep up with my mind,
my limits are stretched far, but not beyond,
and my muscles always ache,
and my mouth always yawns,
does my face crack the mirror,
or was the crack always there,
cause I feel so lazy to fix it,
and my face looks worn and sick,
I just can't keep up with everything anymore,

no...

I don't think one hundred lifetimes would do,

there's far too much on my plate,

for my dreams are bigger than my brain,

as for my body,

I have no energy, and I feel cold and dead,

I'm drained, I'm tired,

and I feel like I'm collapsing,

the ancient pillars have aged over the years,

and my bones,

are not as strong as they once were,

they begin to crumble,

under their own weight from time,

under the strain of day after day,

and no sleep at night,

all my life has been an endurance,

of severe pain,

and there is never any gain,

every day...every week...this passing year...

it's all the same in my eyes, just strain,

backache, headache, and more and more pain,

I try to keep up, to stand on my two feet,
but I just stumble backwards,
I just want to pass out and forever sleep,
any sign of a consciousness, I no longer keep,
my glory days are over, my love and feelings,
are just discarded leftovers,
my empire has collapsed...
and my thoughts have clouded over,
but before the stress of life takes what is left,
of my sanity away from me,
I'm gonna try to accomplish,
at least one more thing today,
those dreams are closer than they appear to me,
but many of them I'll never reach, I'll never see,
most of those dreams,
will never manifest and come to be,
for I have come to the understanding,
that I can only do as much as I can,
with what little time has been given to me...

A place I call my own

~

Out there, past the plains and trees,
over sky and the waves of the sea,
over the mountains and beyond the clouds,
resides a reality, that which I can tolerate,
to a place that's just for me,
and mine to be alone,
where no one can bother me,
and no other voices speak,
except for the thoughts in my mind.

On this hour, bonds and lies of friendship,
have been severed and we're on our own,
I'll be prepared, for I know how to survive,
my instincts are focused and honed,
and I know just where I'm going to go,
to a place that's far away, where I'm all alone,
for none of you shall follow,

for I release all of you, I let all of you go,
survive as you will,
I take on this journey myself,
for I walk alone.

Before me is stretched a long and barren road,
bitter and harsh, for this walk is long and cold,
and standing once again,
upon this gritty asphalt and jagged gravel,
I am a sullen man, who walks alone,
For I am heading for my place,
and by instinct and past hatred,
I know just where I'm going to go.

Beyond the horizons,
of this world I have abandoned,
for I have given up on this life,
and a new life awaits me,
and I know,
as low as existence drives me down below,
at this place I know,

there will be a welcome embrace,

within this sacred place,

I call my one and true home,

a quiet place of rest, a place I can call my own.

wasteLand

~

I feel as though I'm stranded in this wasteland,
chained and bound, naked,
sinking lower and lower in quicksand,
caught in time's pull,
as the hands drag me away,
with the night and day,
slowly in a downwards spiral,
crushed by the mineral within the hourglass,
and if I were to break the crystal and escape,
then I bleed away the time much faster,
and as the sand spirals downwards,
the faster the time expires,
and so will I…so will I…

The wind is harsh all the way down here,
at the bottom of the sub-levels,
the walls are thick,

they keep out the luminous eyes of light,
so no hope can peek in,
and give me a ray, that flicker,
that spark to drive me into the next day,
to start again,
to let me think there may be some hope,
and that the limits the sky,
but the sky is painted on,
an illusion,
to show me something that isn't there,
a ceiling that's not very high,
and it's caving in,
and as this world crumbles all around,
so do I… so do I…

My iron chains keep me bound…
keep me trapped,
not allowing me to move,
not allowing me to run and hide,
these links of solid metal pin me down,
they hold my flesh in place,

keep me out in the open,
to be humiliated by all who pass,
so I imprison myself under sheets,
I curl up in the shadows of my depression,
and the tears begin to fall from my eyes,
effervescent oceans that fall with sadness,
on evaporating skin,
skin that time wears thin,
so fragile and pallid I begin to crack,
my cold body shakes,
and as my flesh breaks apart,
into rubble like bloodless stone,
so do I…so do I…

The snow is building higher,
and the wind is blowing colder,
today, the stitches from my eyes have been cut,
and I open them, I'm waking up,
blinded by these nightmares masticating,
raping my reality, defiling my dreams,
they torture me,

and shovel more dirt into my vision,
for by waking me up,
my grave is just a little bit deeper,
so just let me be,
let me keep dreaming, because I am a sleeper.
I have nowhere I want to go,
there's nowhere I belong,
except to be stuck in this wasteland,
frozen in the moment,
as the time, inch by inch, is ticking,
those two hands waving goodbye,
the lives of those around me, they move on,
they wave goodbye,
oblivious to my tears when I cry,
so I'll just let out one big sigh,
as I kiss this day goodbye,
and close my blood-shot eyes,
sew them back up, and lay back down to sleep,
do not disturb me, I'm at peace, I'm at ease,
my mind is tired, and so am I…so am I…

Before the Moon (Intro)

~

Before the moon….

man appears a man,

but is it the man that becomes the beast?

Or is the beast alive...

has the beast always been,

the true face of man?

When he returns to normal,

will he ever be normal again?

For could it be,

that man is wolf to man….?

Libretto for a Wolv

pt. I

Transformation

~

I feel it coming over me,
this awful, sick feeling is pulsating within,
I can feel my guts twist, my spine snaps and bends,
the nails extend and cut like razors,
my hair grows thick; I sweat, my flesh begins to stink,
like rotten meat that's been left out,
smelling of spoiled food, forgotten in the sink,
that musty smell is suffocating me,
my thoughts of who I am,
are replaced by bestial instincts,
the ticks and mites crawl over my flesh,
they make my skin itch, as they spread their offspring,
and the larvae hatch, deep within the roots of my fur,
they are a parasite for blood,

addicted to the sweet nectar, as am I!
My senses are ten-fold, and the scent of blood,
lingers in the air, as the prey try to hide,
I smell their sweat, the stench of fear,
I hear their breathing, I hear their screaming,
as I corner them, one by one,
and tear them asunder, piece by piece,
man...woman...child...all are my feast!
I tear away the clothes and bury my teeth,
into their flesh, I eat the meat and lick the bones,
but this thing, this shell of a once mortal human being,
this thing is not me, it's just a part of me,
an altered form, a thing that should not exist,
an abomination that preys by night,
and eats his meals, under a full-moon's candlelight.

Libretto for a Wolv

pt. II

Recollection

~

I finally awaken…after a night's debauchery of blood-lust,
I'm naked and cold, lying under the pine trees,
I feel the morning breeze caress over my skin,
my eyes open, but I wish they didn't,
I wish I didn't have to see it, see what I have done again,
I used to be horrified,
but now I'm desensitized and I simply walk away,
I turn a blind eye, to the blood I spilled last night,
the horrid pile of mangled corpses that will be discovered today,
the reporters will be asking, the news will be telling,
the paparazzi will be photographing,
and the papers will be exhibiting,
my altered being is wanted, a celebrity, but I'm in the shadows,

just an ordinary man out walking the streets,
keeping his conscious clean,
but I'm aware…of what I'm capable of,
when the full moon is out,
for I am aware, of the terror that will come out,
there will be more victims, there is no doubt.

Organism

~

...and from the waters, the cellular activity runs rampant,

the microscopes show, a high density, of Oxygen content,

if this thing continues to expand,

its bacteria and cell growth production,

its hunger...will be insatiable,

it's size...more vast and colossal,

than anything that has ever walked,

upon the face of this earth,

the atomic and electrical pulsating conductors,

increases drastically,

through the brain and spinal cord, tightening every muscle,

every ounce of fiber,

to where its reflexes are faster than the speed of light,

this organism,

was not meant for humankind to know of its existence,

for we will be unable to co-exist with its intellectual force,

it will outsmart us, it will hunt us down one by one,
it is neither flesh nor bone,
nor scale or fur.
Is it man? Is it animal? Could it be reptile?
But we were all wrong, it is none of these,
and no...it is not a machine,
for humans build machines,
and this abhor was not of our making,
neither a god, nor a scientist would dare,
to create such a terrible pandemic,
this thing cannot be contained much longer,
it will come for us, you can be sure,
for we are its natural enemy,
this is a world of humans no longer,
its time has come to relieve us of our population and our future,
it will cultivate a new habitat to reign supreme,
as the one true overlord,
our cities will burn, our waters will breed its species,
prepare yourselves, for this is the end of the human beings!

Sally

~

A fair and dainty princess snarling her pincers of skin-devouring mutilation,
mandibles of ancient death absorbing the blood from your poisoned body,
tearing through your hemophiliac flesh.

Nuclear acid taints the tip of her ulcerous, adorably soft, spongy tongue,
caressing upon your skin, the venom pulsates through your nerves to decimate the tissue,
in your brain, with her appetite, there will be no leftovers of your bloody mess.

Her jowls tighten around your head to begin the meal,
from that hard-headed skull,
down to your very last fungus-infected toe,
your skin makes her mouth water, so sweet,

like sugary candy in the light of the moon's glow.

Arising from the depths of the placid, murky waters to gorge
herself on humans, the fat,
ones taste better, filled with juicy warm meat, the skinny ones
are a little too boney and meek,
but the smell of blood is a fragrance of perfume to her rotted
and partially devoured nose.
The young, smaller ones are like little chocolates,
while the larger prey put up a fight,
struggling to survive, and when they taste defeat, her belly
rests easy and she sleeps well,
rested to hunt when the next victim arrives, after masticating
the beef, the bones are disposed.

She smells the red liquid that flows through our veins,
she can feel the fear and,
sense the perspiration that emits from our stinking,
struggling bodies when we try to run,
those crimson eyes can detect our body heat;
she licks her crusty, scaled lips before the feast.

Flesh taste better in the mouth of the beast,

blood runs thicker down the throat of the beast.

"Sally! It's time to eat!"

Weavers

~

There are creatures, a race of beings,
which have been placed here eons ago,
creatures of wisdom and knowledge, and intrigue.

They keep hidden away in their lairs,
away from the light of the sun,
and keep to the shadows of their minds,
and shroud themselves within their thoughts,
and the darkness of their past.

They are the creatures of wisdom,
and on their webs they weave the fate of all,
they counsel those who would brave their inner sanctums,
and delve into the undercrofts of their mountains,
hills, forests, tombs, and temples,
places were most men and women dare not go.

For even though, it is written, that the creatures of wisdom,

are all knowing and all wise, they do however,

require a tribute, an offering to them,

an offering…of flesh and blood.

"...all around the mulberry bush"

~

"All around the mulberry bush

the monkey chased the weasel;

the monkey thought 'twas all in fun..........

.."

A Toy
(Light Version)

~

The glimmer of the tinsel dress,

radiates from the 100 watt light,

sun-kissed across the glimmering bow with a bright streak,

she's ready to be opened,

she's ready for her close up, to be put on display,

threads of blonde hair sashay around her shoulders,

a braid of golden rope like Rapunzel,

her lips glossed with ruby red lipstick,

her rosy plastic cheeks, blush from that first kiss,

she wants to feel love's warmth,

to be embraced in that happy little girl's arms,

a child to take her hand,

a child to be her friend,

BFF's forever, she just needs that someone to love her,

to hold her, to never let her go,

to live the perfect utopian life, that no toy ever could,

an ivory white doll house, she calls her own,
and a doll just like her, a plastic companion,
to play the king, next to her, the queen upon her model throne,
a white picket fence,
insulated walls, doors, and windows, to keep out the cold,
a shingled roof without holes, to conceal them from the rain,
decorated with all the furnishings,
that any little doll needs to be happy,
a dog with faux fur she pats on the head,
a cat with a battery-operated purr, which sits on her lap,
and in the corner, even a tiny little plastic mouse trap,
she has her dresses and jewelry galore,
a smile as wide as glee, a smile sparkling,
what more, could any toy possibly ask for?

A Toy
(Dark Version)

~

As the embers begin to cool around her,
the little doll is left in ruins,
to bathe in black ash,
the little girl no longer remembers, for the little girl,
is a little girl no longer,
jet beads in her eyes ooze of black paint tears,
and the plastic flesh melts with time like candle wax,
and the golden hair, frizzled and charred in the flames
the cobwebs and dust after eons gather,
for they have not returned to claim her,
she has been abandoned, a forgotten memory,
left off the Christmas list this year,
for many more within their packages line the stores,
the dollar and thrift stores that is,
for her kind is wanted no more,
she has no comprehension of the time that has passed,

she lays helpless within her doll house,
now burned down into a twisted,
mangled mess, and that shingled roof has collapsed,
the cat no longer purrs, for the batteries are dead,
and her husband lays in the corner, a mannequin with no head,
the real dog swallowed the faux one, after all,
it is a dog eat dog world,
and that chip on her shoulder remains,
from where she hit the wall,
mistreatment by the hands of that same, sweet little girl,
the saying goes, *"don't bite the hand that feeds!"*
but the smile has decayed, and the lips chipped away,
the right arm dislodged and lost, along with both legs,
under these ruins of the ancient walls,
the carcass of that little girl's doll, will remain,
until the bulldozer comes,
to plow the debris away....

Can't Go Back

~

I can't go back this time,
not now, not ever,
not when I'm ten steps ahead,
why would I want to back again?
For I have so many plans laid before me,
I can't go back to the primitive lands,
for I can't remember,
what life was like back then.
Now, there are so many choices today,
but is it the past were dreambound to?
Do these choices,
really make our dreams come true?
Or is it our hard work now,
that helps us realize what we truly are,
and what were destined to?
We never give ourselves credit,
were credit has been long overdue....

Reoccurring Fantasies

~

The fantasies occur over and over again,
my mind constantly trying to keep up with
these thoughts on a promising idea,
writing about a promised land, going on adventures in places,
that are inconceivable to anyone else,
except for maybe a select few,
but the interpretation is always different,
the plots are never the same,
for some involve a person we love,
for others it's an escape with friends,
an evening out to their rendezvous place,
for me, it's the picture I draw, the story I create,
for me it's the paper and the pen, the perfect couple,
the happiest of unions,
add my mind, my imagination,
and we create the perfect family,

an undying ancestry that will live on in the books, and in film,
for all eternity,
I don't want opinions, because I have my own interpretation,
on how to deal with my troubles and my pain,
I write it all down, and turn it into something fascinating,
for others to interpret and to be entertained,
these ideas don't just happen, how can I explain?
No one understands this feeling, of having a passion,
there is no money or fame involved,
this is something I enjoy doing,
for the concept of story, the conflict between good and evil,
what's right and what's wrong,
these provoking thoughts that move the story along,
this is what drives me,
and to be there,
and witness the reactions on their faces at the very end,
is priceless,
and is worth every ounce of sweat and time,
I put into this process!

For the ideas never stop, they never go away,
my ideas are a part of me, we are one and they are free to stay,
for they never betray, they never judge,
they never cause me distress,
because at the end of the day, my emotions, are at rest,
I wrote everything down,
I'm one with myself, at peace, I'm able to just...relax,
and when I'm feeling down,
my imagination, my thoughts take me back to that special time,
when I was just a boy,
with nothing to lose, and all I needed to be happy,
was all the inspiration that surrounded me,
and my interpretations have made my destiny, a reality...

"Just...Fine"

~

As long as the sky's still blue,
and I have a place,
where I can put my head in the clouds,
I'll be fine.

As long as the sun still rises,
and I feel it's shine,
and the light to brighten my day,
I'll be just fine.

As long as there's something in my life,
that I enjoy doing,
and can get me through the dark times,
I'd say I'm doing fine.

I'm laying down my burdens,
and keeping peace of mind,

I'm enjoying these little moments,
and doing just fine.

I just gotta take things steady,
and move one step at a time,
things will turn out alright,
and I'll be just fine.

As long as we stay true, to who we are inside,
we can't forget, that we're all different,
and truly one of a kind,
we just gotta tough the rough days out,
and we'll turn out just fine.

What brings me down, makes me stronger
I'll be all the wiser,
and I make it home at the end of the day,
after all...I'm still alive,
and that's when I realize,
I'm still doin' fine.

Candle

~

When the day seems to drip away,

and the happiness is melting,

just remember that at the very tip,

a bright flame is burning,

and as long as the happy fire dances,

a flicker of hope is still showing.

The final war…and a new dawn

~

Don't want to feel anger no more,
because I no longer have a need to feel sore,
don't need to settle old scores,
this is my final war.

To let go of discord,
and drain the rage some more,
to be at peace like I was before,
I wage this battle, this is my final war.

All fighting has ceased,
and all the hate from my past,
has been released,
I no longer see those faces with scorn,
I've let go, I've won the final war.

It'll be a new day soon,

and the time moves onward.
We may always look back,
but then we'll never move forward.
A memory is a memory,
but there is a horizon beyond.

Do we dwell on the darkness,
of the night before?
Or awaken to a new dawn,
and start to live once more?
A new day is here,
and we have so much to live for!

Happily Ever After

~

It's all working out for me,

I don't care who loves or hates me,

I've become who I was born to be,

my life has bled,

to use as ink,

and write these thoughts and ideas,

I don't take it back, I wouldn't change anything,

because it's all working out for me,

archaic times, are evolving,

I'm building a civilization,

from the ashes of my past,

I'm a phoenix rising,

my flame of life is continuously sparking,

I don't start new, I continue...I travel onwards,

to see new places, to meet new faces,

my nomadic ways may seem schizophrenic,

but I'm okay with it,

for my curiosity lights these darkened roads,
on the way to discovery,
I have no structure, I have no rules,
no laws do I follow,
I'm not within the bounds,
I'll step over the line, to take the penalty,
I'll strike back to take the foul,
I won't hold back to right what's wrong,
I bet you'll always remember,
I dare you to try and forget,
immortality is what I'm after,
to cement my castle made of sand,
built upon shaky ground, with fragile hands,
but I'll make it stronger,
as my surplus grows larger,
I'll make it better, as I grow older,
my skills I will improve, as I become wiser,
I want to reach the sky,
yet I'm destined to go further,
to reach that goal, to get what I'm truly after,
I'll be gone, but my words will live on forever,

and I can truly say...I know what it means,

to live happily ever after...

I fought like hell

~

I fought like hell this year,

after last year, I thought things could have been better,

but to end with death, and to start again with dying,

many faces I knew, have faded away, passed from sight,

into the endless vaults of time,

where their memories will be forgotten as they slowly decay,

I fought to make things better, and in some ways,

I've succeeded,

but the bad outweighs the good,

no matter how high you stack the chances,

the odds will always win, the tails side of the coin has landed,

I guess I made more mistakes, the more I took the chances,

I guess I made the wrong choices, I picked heads every time,

and tails has always landed,

I guess I never learn from my mistakes,

but I won't give up, I must try harder,

I've had relationships break,

made friendships which could have lasted forever,
but crumbled in the palm of my fist,
and I open my hand, the ashes of all the yesterdays,
blows away with tomorrow's wind,
and at the stroke of midnight, on the eve of the new year...
I'll just sigh, pondering if I'm able to continue,
because there are no redo's,
I guess it's that time again,
as another year comes, that means another has to die,
I fought like hell this year,
I guess it's time to learn from the past this time,
but can I?
I guess I can give it another try...

Party's Over

~

Sweaty and putrid, my body stained with blood,
I look all around me, where is everyone? Is the party done?
The masks lay upon pale, lifeless faces collapsed on the floor,
the smell of piss and alcohol lingers in the cool autumn breeze,
I need to crack the windows and release that smell,
but the windows are gone!
Puke and bile stains the curtains and decorative rugs,
tongues within decayed mouths have been disintegrated by the
riptide of regurgitated stomach acid,
and the enamel of teeth whittled away,
"It's a shame!" Their dentist would say to them,
their doctor would be speechless,
without diagnosis to their cause of death,
except a clue might be the strong smell
of ethanol upon their breath.

I look around at the men and women, passed out?

No...they're dead on the floor,
The wet dreams have stained undesirable women,
by unwanted men,
What happened last night? Too many meds...?
And all went black, the masquerade is over!
Boy, my head is throbbing by the bright light shining in,
is it the sun?
No, I think I might be dead!
Speaking of death, whose blood is this that stains my hands?
Is it the woman lying next to me, who lies motionless,
bathed in this stench of my making,
my foulness, my unrelenting force upon her fragile body!
I remove her mask, to see her face...nope...I don't know her,
I don't remember,
that special moment we shared together.

Can someone please...tell me what happened last night!
For all turned black, at the stroke of midnight,
we all fell under the spell of the witching hour!
This isn't my house...this isn't my bed...too many meds,
must have gone to my head.

What was I doing...what did I say?!
There are no clues, I have no memories stashed away,
what did we do...what did we say, how did this happen?
What brought about this fate?

I get up to walk, but my knees hit the hardwood floor, I crawl,
I drag my paws across the floor, like a dog,
I crawl upon all fours,
over bodies, over limp arms and legs, faces expressionless,
terrified by the last thing they had seen,
for whatever killed them...
could it...could it have been...?
Why am I the only survivor? Why am I still alive?!
I don't know what happened, or why everyone else has died!
Whose house is this? Did he or she, or they,
approve of this masquerade?
My mask is still on, and my body lithe and pallid,
naked and trapped in the cold wind,
I see the living quarters ahead of me, will I make it?
Crawling upon my hands and knees,
while I'm here I might as well beg for mercy.

The ballroom floor is soaked with blood,
and there's a dripping sound, *"drip...drip"*
I look above, and my eyes behold, for I wish they lied.

I see the bodies of thousands, they are strung up so high,
and it's their blood that drips to the
floor, from deep gashes, and bruised sores.
At their ankles, they are bound upside down by rustic chains,
hooks driven deep into the soft part of their feet.
And the only sounds are the sounds of the autumn wind...
and their crimson blood raining down,
"drip...drip...drip..."
The chandelier has fallen from the ceiling,
Lucifer's torch has hit the final circle, for within this room,
once a dance floor, is now the remains of a lifeless desolation,
the icicles of light lay scattered and smashed across the
polished, hardwood floor,
splattered over human bones and pierced flesh,
cut by Lucifer's glass.
The library has been ripped to pieces, ancient books and tomes
scattered about, burned and decimated,

the scent of gasoline is thick in this room,
this room has been burned by flames, the
ancient playwrights and authors of old, burned like witches,
for nothing but the ashes of their work remains,
sprinkled upon the charred rug.
The upstairs has caved in,
the ceiling now nothing more than a gaping hole,
looking up at the sky,
to a fiery orange dawn engulfing all in its blaze,
for there is no sun to be seen, it has been decimated,
and only a poisoned atmosphere,
of nitrogen gas and sulfur, is all that remains.
The stairs of stone and carved marble have crumbled,
so it seems my chance to ascend upwards has long passed,
"am I...am I really the Last?!"

I take off my mask...or at least I try, but it sticks to my flesh,
it burns...it burns as I pull it,
for the skin and plastic have fused together as one,
bound by heat and radiation, it peels off,
but as I tear the mask away,

the thought occurs to me...that this mask...is it my true face?
So it seems these terrible truths and lies,
I was never able to mask or hide.
I can feel my cheek bones, it is my skull that my fingers caress!
My skull has been exposed, my true face,
the monster that lays beneath this flesh,
my true face...is my mask,
and the terror beneath is now exposed!
But is this horrible twisted disfigurement I feel,
a skull? or is this the face of a starved man,
a deprived man, stripped of all his pleasures from the night
before, as punishment, for these terrible atrocities,
these crimes against all humanity?!
Could it...could it have been...?

The clenched stomach beneath my exposed ribs,
growls and gurgles,
for how can one even think of eating,
when one walks on the fringe,
between the living, and the dead?
Walks alone in a world,

were massive extinction and genocide has spread?
When have I last eaten, was there a feast?
Was there dining and wine the night before?
I hate to say...but I think I found my answer,
for piled in the corner of the dining room,
twenty, fifty, maybe more,
chewed up bodies and sliced carcasses, exposed limbs,
with the veins and arteries,
still wrapped around the gristle and bones, a horror to behold,
for I dare not say anymore,
for I cannot recall the taste of flesh,
or the swill nectar of blood rushing down my throat,
but upon the dining table before my eyes,
are carved pieces of human meat,
with the skin and hair still attached, which parts,
it's impossible to say for sure,
it's all meshed and mangled together on dinner plates,
and in soup bowls,
cut with knives, stuck with forks, and scooped out with spoons,
eyes float within the chalices and goblets,
entrails mixed with the soufflé,

to give it that extra taste,
bone marrow pressed into cake as filling,
iced with moist brains,
splattered by bull-peen hammers, crushed into a moist paste,
rotating by mechanisms and leavers of some odd contraption,
over the fire pit,
roasts the livers, kidneys, and spleens...to perfection,
a crisp golden brown cuisine.
But did we wash the vegetables, the lettuce and the tomatoes,
the basil and herbs?
Everyone knows that meat is best garnished with fresh,
crisp greens.

The kitchen is a wreck,
nobody cleaned their dishes or swept up the cake crumbs,
and now the tiny bodies of roaches and rats lay rotting
everywhere,
dead by the traps, or by fighting one another,
fighting for their fill,
for the last one standing,
will be the god of all the waste left over,

"...Am I the god of all this waste left over? Am I the god now?
and this my kingdom-come to rule over?
To oversee all these bodies of,
human and pest, persons alike, animals and their fleas?"
What will we tell the authorities?
Nobody even bothered to clean up,
their part at the scene of the crime!
"...but was it them? Or...or could it have been...?"
They wouldn't stop to ask questions, they'd just shoot us,
one by one we would fall, dead on sight,
"...is that what happened?"
there would be no trial, for there are no more judges,
no jury, no more laws exist,
but...but I still exist, and I have no laws to follow,
there is no they, no us...there are none but me...
I stand here alone,
what happened to everyone, what happened to this place,
what happened to everything?

I get to my feet, I take a robe from that corpse over there,
he no longer needs it, he's dead and cold...but I...

I'm alive and naked,
a burning sweat drenches my fevered body,
and the black velvet seems,
with an odd sensation, it soothes my cracked, parched skin;
it's a natural fit.
The door to this palace, the manor has been shattered,
pieces of wood, splinters are scattered about,
my feet are cut and pierced by glass,
and those splinters as I walk,
my legs are in shambles, with a decrepit limp,
as I move across this charred,
ballroom floor, blackened by flames,
to a polished ebony finish.

I go outside, into the noxious air, that cold autumn breeze,
is the icy hand of death,
as he glides across the sky upon a steed with black wings,
his ebony robes flutter in the wind,
as he grips the sickle of Father Time,
tighter in his grasp, but this figure, this icon of life's end,
he looks down upon me,

and laughs at this desolation of mankind,
this raping of the earth, and he points his finger...
he points his icy finger at me,
and then he uncovers his hood, and beneath the shadows,
he is not as I have always seen him before,
in pictures and on film,
for he is a man, a man of flesh and blood, eyes and hair,
someone with a face and teeth,
but what is uncovered,
what was hidden beneath that black hood, is now revealed,
for death has shown his true face today,
for the face he wears...is my face...it's...it's me!
For now the truth is told, for death has a name, and that name,
is my name, for I am the destroyer, the bringer of pain,
the cause of all these atrocities, the slayer, the slaughterer,
the ending of all things, for now...I understand my answer...
There were no meds involved, nor alcoholic remedies,
just these crazy thoughts within my head.
I have waged my war, my genocide, my revenge,
a cover up as a masquerade,
for I invited them in, and I have killed them all,

none were spared,
I eliminated them...they have been done away with,
they were all slayed!
but you...all but you, and so I turn to you.

I see you now! You thought you could hide from me,
as I look down upon you,
from my steed that flies on black wings,
but my shadow has spread, and the night, is now my daylight,
for I see all that moves within my darkness, my line of sight,
for none can hide within this nether world, this apocalypse,
this darkside of my mind, for you have ran,
you ran as much as you could, as far as you could go,
but now, there is no place left to go, nowhere to hide,
for within my mind, your life is forfeit,
when you chose to enter this place,
you cast yourself down to the floor on your hands and knees,
a beggar,
but you will get no mercy, no love, no respect,
for peace is but the broken wings of a black dove,
crippled and useless, impaired within this altered state of being,

this crumbled civilization, only a check point,
the last exit before you reach insanity,
your own mental breakdown and self-destruction,
for that...is your destiny,
for I hold your being, in the palm of my black hand,
just one squeeze, and you cease to be...but!
Maybe we can parley, maybe we could barter,
maybe I could tempt you,
with a proposition, for I need someone to spread my words,
to spread my lies,
a martyr to wear this mask, and guide others,
into this realm...the abyss of sadism,
that lingers in the back of my mind,
for are you still with me, if you're on my side, and do as I ask?
I just might let you live long enough...to witness the rebirth,
of a new mankind!
And we bury the charred remains, of what's left of the past.

"...and so,

when it all comes down in the end and the candlelight dims...

soon to be nothing more, than a puff of smoke taken away,

by the wind...."

www.ingramcontent.com/pod-product-compliance
Lightning Source LLC
Chambersburg PA
CBHW031444040426
42444CB00007B/967
* 9 7 8 0 6 1 5 9 4 8 7 4 4 *